Kids & Computers

The First Computers

Charles A. Jortberg

Published by Abdo & Daughters, 4940 Viking Drive, Suite 622, Edina, Minnesota 55435.

Copyright © 1997 by Abdo Consulting Group, Inc., Pentagon Tower, P.O. Box 36036, Minneapolis, Minnesota 55435 USA. International copyrights reserved in all countries. No part of this book may be reproduced in any form without written permission from the publisher.

Printed in the United States.

Cover and Interior Photo credits: Wide World Photos
　　　　　　　　　　　　　　　　　Archive Photos
　　　　　　　　　　　　　　　　　Jortberg Associates
　　　　　　　　　　　　　　　　　Super Stock
　　　　　　　　　　　　　　　　　Bettmann Archive
Edited by John Hamilton

Library of Congress Cataloging-in-Publication Data

Jortberg, Charles A.
　　　The first computers / Charles A. Jortberg.
　　　p. cm. -- (Kids and computers)
　　　Includes index.
Summary: Surveys the history of devices leading up to modern computer systems, from ancient celestial calculators and abacuses to punched card systems and the Univac.
ISBN 1-56239-723-0
1. Computers--History--Juvenile literature. [l. Computers--History.] I. Title. II. Series
Jortberg, Charles A. Kids and computers.
QA76.52.J673 1997
681'.14--dc20
　　　　　　　　　　　　　　　　96-28295
　　　　　　　　　　　　　　　　　CIP
　　　　　　　　　　　　　　　　　AC

About the Author

Charles A. Jortberg graduated from Bowdoin College in 1951 with a Bachelor's Degree in Economics. Mr. Jortberg joined IBM in 1954 and served in several capacities. Among his assignments were coordinating all of IBM's efforts with the Air Force, managing a 20-person team of IBM engineers, and directing a number of technical programs at NASA's Electronic Research Laboratory. He formed Jortberg Associates in 1972, where he currently works, to provide an outlet for his start up technology experience.

Contents

The Early Systems

The history of inventions leading up to the modern computer is a story of people striving to create machines that automate many tasks that today we take for granted, such as adding up long strings of numbers, controlling airplanes in flight, or helping surgeons locate tumors. Many of the earliest methods of recording and counting data are shrouded in mystery. In England you can visit Stonehenge, where a mysterious collection of large stones have stood since 1,500 B.C. Scientists have never discovered the stones' purpose. However, by observing the way the sun shines between the stones, many people believe Stonehenge was used to predict the seasons and eclipses of the sun and the moon.

Another early method of computing was a brass calculator, which existed in Spain nearly 1,000 years ago. The machine was shaped like a human head, with numbers instead of teeth. The shape became its undoing; a group of priests was afraid the machine was supernatural, and destroyed it.

In early recorded history, calculators that used the sun, or objects in the night sky, were developed to help early navigators explore the world beyond the Tigris-Euphrates Valley of southwestern Asia. One such device, traced to the first century, was recovered from a sunken ship near Greece. It worked with a system of gears designed to track the orbits of stars and planets. These orbits became the marked routes for ocean-going vessels.

In ancient Rome and Greece, one of the earliest machines ever used for processing numbers was the abacus. This simple collection of beads has been used for centuries in China and other Asian countries. The abacus is built with columns of beads attached to a rectangular wooden frame. Inside the wooden frame is a crossbar that separates each column of beads into two sections. In the Chinese version there are two beads above the bar and five below. Each bead below the bar means one, and each bead above means five. By pushing the beads toward the bar, the beads can be combined to represent numbers. For example,

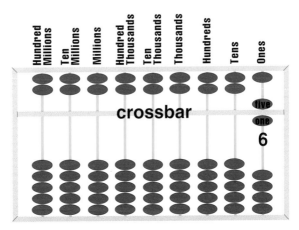

On the abacus, the number 6 is represented by a One bead and a Five bead on the Ones wire.

if one bead above the bar (five) is pushed against it, and one below the bar (one) is pushed against it, this equals a total of six.

Each column of beads meant a different range of numbers. The first column represents ones, the second tens, the third hundreds, etc. With a number of columns, numbers in the billions can be shown. By shifting beads, addition, subtraction, multiplication, and division are quickly completed. Because values are shown by positions, the abacus is very valuable in teaching arithmetic to blind students.

Experienced users operate the abacus very quickly. After World War II, a speed contest was arranged in Japan between the fastest calculator operator in the U.S. Army and an employee of the Japanese Post Office using an abacus. The American was defeated easily by the shifting beads of his opponent.

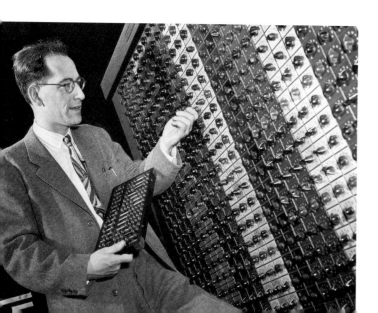

Dr. John Mauchly holds an abacus while standing in front of the earliest adding machine, the ENIAC.

Charles Babbage

Although the computer as we know it didn't exist until the 1940s, there were two men who lived in the 1800s who had a strong influence on these machines. The first man was Charles Babbage. He was born in England in 1792 and is recognized as the father of the modern computer. This is really amazing since the first one wasn't built until 150 years after Babbage was born.

Babbage was considered a genius at a very young age. By the time he was 19, he advised the leading mathematicians in England. He was also very curious, and loved to invent things. One of his inventions is the "cow catcher," a sloping piece of metal on the front of train locomotives designed to throw objects off the track before the train hit them.

Another of Babbage's inventions is the modern concept of our postal system. His idea was to charge the same amount for mailing a letter no matter where in England it was going. This was a big improvement over the old system, where every letter could cost a different amount. The same principle is used today in the United States.

In 1830 Babbage designed a machine called the "Analytical Engine." It became the basis of most modern computers. The design called for a huge machine—a complex collection of gears, shafts, and chains—to be run by a steam engine. Money for the project was provided by the English government, but halfway through construction funding was halted, and the machine was never finished.

The whole idea of the "Analytical Engine" would have been lost if it weren't for a woman who worked with Babbage. Lady Ada Byron wrote down everything that Babbage planned for the machine.

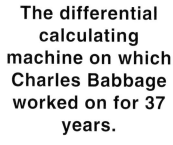

The differential calculating machine on which Charles Babbage worked on for 37 years.

She also wrote out detailed mathematical steps the "engine" would follow to solve a problem. Because of her work, some people call Lady Byron the first computer programmer. Her notes were very complete and were used over 100 years later to teach people the principles of the stored-program computer. Her ability to write came naturally, since her father was Lord George Gordon Byron, the famous British poet.

Charles Babbage, mathematician and inventor of the calculating machine.

Joseph Jacquard

The second person from the 1800s who influenced the development of computers was a cloth weaver from France named Joseph Jacquard. In the early 1800s, it was almost impossible for weavers to duplicate patterns. The different color threads had to be inserted into the weaving machine at exactly the same place so the cloth would look the same each time.

Jacquard invented a loom with wooden paddles or cards

French inventor Joseph Marie Jacquard (1752-1834).

punched with holes. Only certain wires passed through the holes, which controlled the loom. To prove to skeptics how well the card system worked, Jacquard made a large piece of cloth with his portrait woven into it. Then he had the portrait woven again—and it looked exactly the same as the first. Babbage planned to use these punched paddles to store information and to read it into his "engine."

After the demonstration, weavers in France threatened to kill Jacquard because they were afraid the loom would put them out of work. But the loom actually created *more* jobs. The Jacquard loom was soon recognized as a major improvement in the weaving industry—more than 11,000 of them were installed in France alone.

Original model of the loom invented by Joseph Jacquard, utilizing punched cards.

The American Connection

In the 1890s, the first American influence was felt in the world of computing. One of the early inventors was a young bank clerk named William Burroughs, who was tired of the drudgery of adding thousands of accounts by hand. For more than 20 years he worked on a machine that could add, subtract, multiply, and divide—and print the results. His inventions were the first products of a company that would become one of the giants of the computer industry. Burroughs, the company that bore his name, eventually joined the Univac company, which one day became the Unisys company. Burroughs died at the young age of 41.

Punched Card Systems

Around the turn of the century Herman Hollerith, a young man working for the U.S. Bureau of the Census, came up with some ideas that would greatly change the way businesses kept records. According to U.S. law, a complete census must be taken every four years. Every man, woman, and child in the country must be counted.

Census numbers are very important, since they are used to figure out all sorts of things, like where members of Congress come from. The number of members of the House of Representatives from each state depends on its population. For example, New York would have more members of Congress than Alaska because more people live in New York. Because so many people move from state to state, it is important to recount the population every four years.

Herman Hollerith, inventor of the punched card system; developed tabulating machines for the United States Bureau of Census.

Many years ago, census counts were done by hand with the aid of some adding and bookkeeping machines. It was a never-ending job. Many times the counting wasn't finished before the next census was taken.

The census of 1880 took over seven years to complete. By the time it was finished, the information was too old to be of real value. While on a leave of absence from his job, Hollerith took classes at the Massachusetts Institute of Technology. After talking to his teachers he got an idea for a machine that would speed up the counting.

Hollerith used the same approach for storing information that Jacquard had used with his loom. He stored information on small cards used for adding, subtracting, multiplying, dividing, and printing. But instead of printing the information on the cards, he recorded the information by punching holes in the cards. Each hole represented a different number. For example, if the hole was punched near the top of the card, it meant that a number one was stored, and if the hole was at the bottom it meant a nine was stored. He even invented a method that stored all the letters of the alphabet in punched holes in the card.

When Hollerith was deciding how big to make the card, he chose an American dollar bill, since it is such a common piece of paper. (Back then, the dollar bill was a little larger than the ones used today.) Each card was divided into eighty columns that ran the width of the card. Each column could be punched with one number or one letter so each card could "store" 80 numbers or letters. The holes were punched by a machine called a "key punch." A person sat at the machine and used a keyboard that looked like a typewriter, with each number and letter having its own key. When a key was pressed the machine punched a hole in the card in the correct position. For example, to punch the name "John Smith," the machine punched holes in four columns for "John." It left a space between the names, and then punched five columns for the name "Smith."

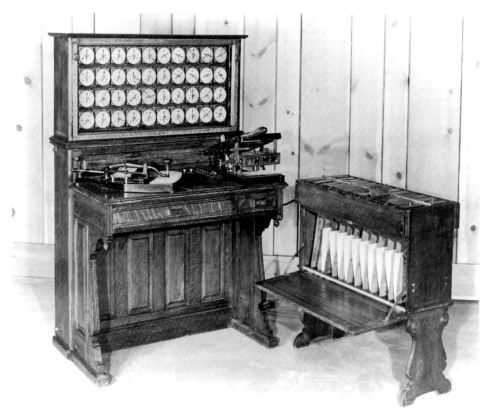

The Hollerith tabulator-sorter box.

Once information was punched in the cards, machines could use the cards for adding, subtracting, multiplying, and dividing. Other machines sorted the cards and printed out the information from them. The card sorters were built with several rollers that moved the cards over a long path that looked like a conveyor belt. Under this conveyor were several small compartments that looked like open-ended mailboxes—one for each of the numbers 0 to 9.

The cards were stacked like a big deck of playing cards. A roller grabbed one card and passed it under a copper brush that looked like a small paintbrush. If the copper brush fell through a hole and touched a metal roller, it created an electrical connection, like a light switch being turned on. This electrical connection would open a door at the top of one of the compartments. When the card reached the compartment it would fall into it.

After all the cards passed through the sorter, the cards with a 1 punched in a certain column would be in one pocket, all the 2s in the next pocket, and so on. Early card sorters could sort 50 cards per minute. Eventually, newer machines were sorting cards at over 1,000 per minute.

A tabulating machine.

Counting and Printing

Once information was punched in the cards and they had been sorted, the cards were then put into an accounting machine, which had the same kind of copper brushes as the sorting machines. This time, the numbers from the cards went to a location called a counter. The counters were used to add or subtract the numbers from several cards.

In the census, accounting machines were used to keep a count of all the people whose names had been punched in the cards. In addition to the people's names, the cards had numbers that stood for the cities where they lived. The census could count the people in Boston by sorting the cards and selecting all of the cards that were punched with Boston's number. All of these cards then fell into the same compartment in the sorter. Finally, they were put into the accounting machines and added. The accounting machines could also print the information from the cards and the answers from the counters.

A vertical sorting machine.

Calculating

While the accounting machines were very useful in adding, subtracting, and printing information, they could not multiply or divide very easily. Punched card calculators were designed to perform these important steps. In these machines the same type of copper brushes were used to read the information into the machine.

For example, to multiply number "A" times number "B," the information punched in card "A" was read into a counter. Numbers punched in card "B" were read into another counter. The calculator would then multiply the information in the "A" counter by the information in the "B" counter, and the answer could then be put into another counter called "C." The machine would then punch the answer into the card in a place called "C."

Suppose you had a job mowing lawns, and you were paid $3.00 per hour. Here's how a punched card calculator figured out how much you earned in a week: One set of columns would be called "Hourly Rate," in which 3.00 was punched. In another group of columns, called "Hours," was punched the total hours you worked—20. The calculator read the 3.00 into one counter, the 20 into another counter, multiplied the two, and the answer, 60, would be found in another counter. This answer would then be punched into the same card location "C." If you wanted to see how much you made in a year, all the cards with these amounts could then be put into an accounting machine and the whole year added up and printed.

In these punched card calculators you decided what you wanted to calculate and then wired the steps into a control panel that was inserted into the side of the machine. Each task you wanted to perform was called a "step." Most of the early punched card calculators could perform only 60 program steps (compared to today's computers, which can work with thousands of steps).

Other Devices

Other developments in the punched card era were transferred later to computers. Many of them are used today in some form. Among these is something called "mark sensing." This is done with special locations on the card printed with areas that look like little boxes. In many cases there is a box for each number from 0 to 9. If you want to enter the number 1234, you fill in these boxes with a special pencil. A machine reads the pencil marks and punches the correct holes for 1234. Today, this type of reading is now done with the marks being read, but instead of punching holes, the numbers enter a computer memory. In schools many tests are marked this way, and in some cities and towns election ballots are counted with a mark-sensing system.

Other machines in the punched card era included reproducers, which automatically made copies of large groups of cards. If you had a stack of cards with information on each student in your school, and you wanted to send it to some other location, you wouldn't want to punch all those cards again by hand. With a reproducer you put the old cards in one side and a stack of blank cards in another. The machine then reads the holes and punches the blank cards exactly the same way. When you were done you had two sets that were exactly the same.

This machine was the largest calculator of its time, weighing three tons, containing 75,000 parts. It was built at the University of Pennsylvania, 1935.

Early Stored-Program Computers

Thanks to the punched card system, the Census of 1890 took only two and a half years to count, instead of seven years for the previous census. Punched card systems became a huge success, and were used in thousands of companies to keep track of information. As a big supplier of punched card machines, IBM became one of the largest companies in the world. Another successful punched-card supplier was Remington Rand.

When World War II broke out, the need for up-to-date information grew quickly. There were new weapons to design, thousands of soldiers and sailors to keep track of, and new ways were needed to send information over telephone lines in code. There was a rush to build machines that could give answers faster than the punched card systems could deliver.

A stored-program computer is a computer in which the steps needed to solve a problem are stored in the computer's memory. This is different from the punched card machines, in which the steps were stored in the control panel. Efforts to build stored-program computers went forward, with the Germans getting an early start. A German inventor, Konrad Zuse, designed a computer early in the war that would have been very useful in developing new weapons. Thankfully for the United States and its allies, the German military didn't push for widespread use of the Zuse machine.

Meanwhile, the Germans were sending all of their messages and orders to army and navy units over radio and telephone lines. They invented a special machine called an Enigma, which coded these messages so that only a person with another Enigma could unscramble the codes.

The English were able to steal an Enigma machine without the Germans knowing they had it. Using the captured machine, young British scientist Alan Turing helped design a huge computer named Colossus. Ten were eventually built. After thousands of hours, the Colossus machines were able to break the German code. From then on every message sent to the German armies, navy ships, and submarines could be intercepted and decoded, helping the Allies figure out what the Germans were going to do next. The Colossus computer was so secret that only a few people knew about it until after the war.

After the war, Turing received a medal from the English government for his contribution to the victory over Germany. He designed several computers after the war, and in 1950 predicted that someday computers would be built that could think. Turing died in 1954. Many people think he would have been very pleased when the big IBM computer beat a world chess champion in the first of a series of games.

The 082 Sorter by IBM.

At Harvard University in the United States, scientist Howard Aiken directed the development of a computer called the Mark I. The machine was very big, with more than 3,000 switches that were used in calculations. The machine would help the U. S. Navy aim the big guns on ships. The navy had to figure out the path of the shells from these guns so they could be aimed correctly. This path was called the shells' "trajectory." For each gun, the navy had to calculate how much powder to use and how high to aim if they wanted the shell to go a certain distance. As new guns were produced, the Mark I computers could do these calculations in minutes, while the old methods took weeks.

A bank of Mark I perceptron units at Cornell University.

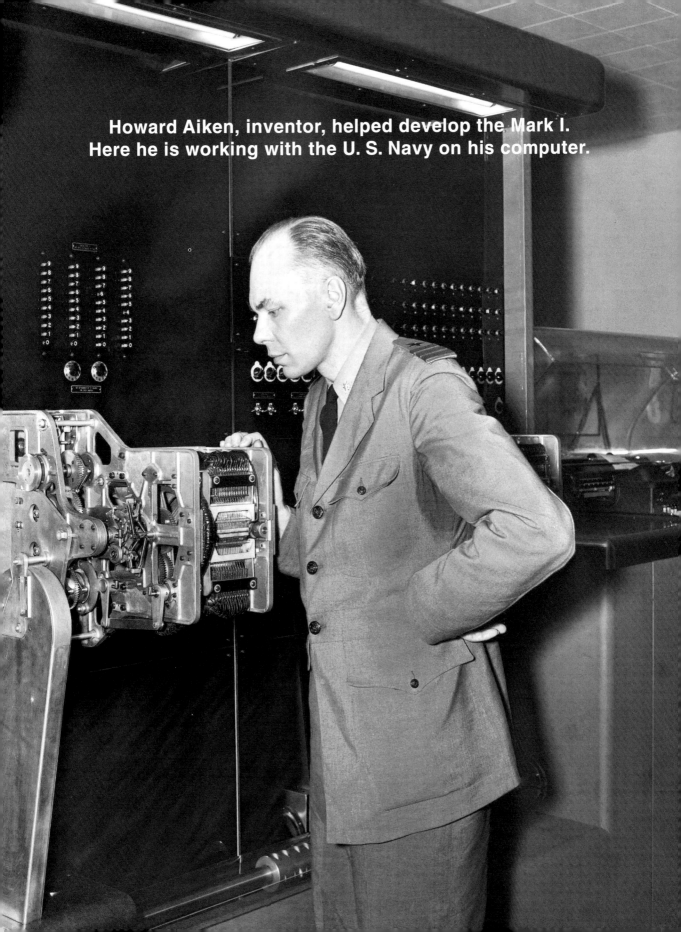

Howard Aiken, inventor, helped develop the Mark I.
Here he is working with the U. S. Navy on his computer.

IBM's Big Machines

In 1946 two Americans, John Mauchly and J. Presper Eckert, designed one of the first electronic-stored-program computers. Working at the University of Pennsylvania, they built a gigantic machine called the ENIAC. It weighed 30 tons, was 18 feet tall, and 80 feet long.

It contained more than 500 miles of wire, and used so much electricity all the lights in the neighborhood dimmed. Although ENIAC was much faster than the older systems, the computer had to be rewired to solve every different problem. This rewiring often took days. Mauchly and Eckert followed the ENIAC with another big machine, and then formed their own computer company.

Above: General view of the ENIAC calculating machine. Opposite page: Dr. Eckert in front of the control panel of the machine he helped design called the ENIAC, 1946.

One of Mauchly and Eckert's big computer designs soon caught the attention of the Remington Rand Company. This company had sold its own punched card systems, which were similar to IBM's products. After Remington Rand bought the Eckert and Mauchly computer company, they developed a large computer that could be used in business. The machine became known as the Univac.

Dr. Mauchly, co-inventor of the ENIAC, sets function tables to solve a mathematical problem.

In the first showing of a computer at work on television, the Univac was used to predict a presidential election. The name Univac was soon used by people to describe any computer. Years later Remington Rand changed its company name to Univac.

Dr. John von Neumann helped perfect electronic computers with his mathematical calculations.

Another important contributor to early computer development was Princeton professor John von Neumann. He invented a computer that used its memory to store the instructions, or program steps. Instead of rewiring the computer for each new job, program steps could be read into memory by having the instructions punched into cards. The cards could then be read into the computer. This design allowed the same computer to be set up for a new problem in only minutes. Because of its ability to work on many different problems, this machine became known as a "general purpose" computer. Most of today's computers are designed the same way as the von Neumann machines.

Even though these new computers made headlines, few experts believed that there would be much practical use for them. After all, they were so big and complicated that you had to be a genius to run them. A vice president of IBM predicted that there would only be 100 computers used worldwide. How very wrong he was.

Glossary

abacus - One of the earliest devices ever used for processing numbers.

accounting - The system, practice, or occupation of recording, managing, or examining financial records or accounts.

accounting machine - An important punched card machine that stored information from the key punched cards and produced printed reports.

bookkeeping - The work or system of keeping records of business accounts or transactions.

card sorters - A machine that sorts punched cards.

celestial bodies - Galaxies, stars, planets, moons, and other satellites in space.

census - An official count of people in a country or district, made in order to obtain certain statistics, such as age, sex, occupation, or economic status.

Colossus - A secret computer used by the British army to unscramble the codes that the German Army sent on the "Enigma."

computer - An electronic device that performs complex mathematical calculations quickly, using information and instructions it receives and stores.

electronic-stored-program computer - A computer that stores programs and data electronically.

ENIAC - A gigantic machine designed by John Mauchly and J. Presper Eckert that was the first electronic-stored program computer.

Enigma - A machine used by the German Army that created special codes that only another "Enigma" machine could receive and translate into words.

general purpose computer - A computer that used its memory to store the instructions, and can work on many different kinds of problems at once.

loom - A machine for weaving thread into cloth.

mark sensing - A way of reading special cards that had little boxes filled in with pencil. When scanned through the computer, the answers were directly put into the computer's memory.

program - A series of coded instructions used to direct a computer in the solution of a problem.

programmer - A person who programs a computer.

punched card calculator - A machine that can multiply or divide information using punched cards.

punched card system - A system that uses punched cards to store information and computer programs.

stored-program computer - A computer that stores programs internally without the need of punched cards.

trajectory - The curved path followed by a missile, bullet, meteor, or the like, moving through space or the atmosphere.

Univac - One of the first big computers that could be used by businesses.

Index